I0079477

THE BONSAI CURATOR

Copyright © 2013 by Pamela L. Laskin

All rights reserved. No part of this book may be reproduced in any manner without written consent except for the quotation of short passages used inside of an article, criticism, or review.

Červená Barva Press
P.O. Box 440357
W. Somerville, MA 02144-3222

www.cervenabarvapress.com

Bookstore: www.thelostbookshelf.com

Production Intern: Kate Clavet

Cover Art: "Rain" by Bertha Lum, Brooklyn Museum (1908)

Cover Design: William J. Kelle

ISBN: 978-0-9883713-5-4

Library of Congress Control Number: 2013933522

Distributed by Small Press Distribution: www.spdbooks.org

ACKNOWLEDGMENTS

Acknowledgment is given to the following publications in which these poems appeared or will soon be appearing.

"Charades," "Masks," and "Schizophrenic Mother,"
AWAKENINGS REVIEW
"Cross Country Skiing," *BRISTLECONE*
"A Tale," *DRIFTWOOD*
"Constant Chronic," *MINNETONKA REVIEW*
"The Abortion," *NEW YORK QUARTERLY*
"Dear Hades," *POEMS THAT THUMP IN THE DARK*
"A Yoga Lesson," "On the Eve of Halloween," "Satsuki Azalea,"
POETRY IN PERFORMANCE
"The Bonsai Curator," *PROMETHEAN*
"Dwarfed, Losses," *THE ONE THREE EIGHT*
"Hurricane Andrew," *SIDEWALKS*

A significant portion of the poems in this book have been published in *World Audience*.

Acknowledgment is given to the following book, which I used for much of my research: Liang, Professor Amy.
THE LIVING ART OF BONSAI. Sterling Publishing Co., Inc. New York.

To Ira, who has always helped me grow!

TABLE OF CONTENTS

1. IN THE MUSEUM, INTO THE WOODS:
History, Care, Neglect

II. OUT OF THE MUSEUM, INTO THE WORLD

THE BONSAI CURATOR

1.

IN THE MUSEUM, INTO THE WOODS:
History, Care and Neglect

Bonsai Beauty

I have been birthed/unearthed
from air,

a mutation
my odd, atrophied limbs
are startling.

Like a fixture I stand
paralyzed
by motherless memories.

Yes, there is a tree here
but at fifty
I still can't grow.

A History

Pen-tsai
during the Chin dynasty
became "tree pen-ching"
during the Yuan dynasty;
pen-ching during the Ching dynasty,
and finally,
bonsai
translated by the Japanese
from the Chinese
during the T'ang dynasty.

The lesson teaches
art is more natural
than nature,
 far from the truth
that tells us:
manipulation is always a menace
especially at the hands
of a mother.

Palm of an Immortal

"The mists of three peaks are in the hands of an immortal."
Sung Tun-P'o, Sung Dynasty Poet

The containers
for those beauties
are white
 or green porcelain,
now in the collection
at the National Palace museum
in Taipei.
Without regard
to the "little child scenes"
that desire nothing more
than to shatter their safety
to smithereens.

The Monk

Miniature bonsai
even more reduced in size
during the Yuan dynasty
when Yun Sang-jen, a monk
visited famous mountains and rivers
for his "little child scenes."

The pines, bamboo and plum trees
were friends,
siblings,
from the same father,
a recluse
who made his children lovely,
but lonely.

Wretchedly Loved

Who wouldn't want
to escape the forest?
Those regal redwoods
tower so tall
(surely they've known heaven),
even the maples,
their gloved, velveteen hands
brazen and beautiful.

Why not
be a bonsai,
and hibernate
away from the others?
To revel
in aloneness
 uniqueness,
and be indulged
by one owner
who says,
"You never have to leave;
I will bathe you
and twist your roots
 perfectly;
no comparisons
not even a growth chart
to follow--
forever little
and wretchedly loved."

Bonsai Curator

I am the curator
 of bonsais
(Is there a curator of bonsais?)

I don't know,
but I'll be one
anyway.

I am good
at stunting growth.
I've kept myself
five forever.

I don't ever leave home
and live in my mother's
museum of darkness

where tainted tapestries
and French provincial chairs
speak of another century

when daughters hid behind the drapes
of mother's dresses
and mothers smiled malignantly

at the miniature trees
thriving in their tiny dungeons,

and I smiled, too
because I am one of them.

Scars

Choosing a good root base is important,
one with vigorous and shallow surface roots
that radiate outward evenly,
so is the trunk base
which should be the shape of a trumpet.

All of this
supposedly ensures superior bonsais,
yet even these
have hidden scars
from cuts on the trunk
sometimes invisible.

The outside is beautiful,
the inside, treacherous.

Masks

"I wore a mask and my face grew to fit it." George Orwell

She couldn't get rid of the smile—
big, red,
fixed
like a tattoo
on raw skin
bruised
in childhood.

The world saw smiles
while she felt sorrow
breaking, budding out
of her blemished face.

She forgot what it was like
inside skin,
as she moved—stiff and hard
like an empty casket.

Charades

No more charade.
Don't ask me to play
daughter
to a mother
who made me disappear
when I was five.

One Halloween
you said,
"be a ghost"
and threw me a sheet
like a diaper
to keep it inside.

It didn't work.
Skin
was a veil
to these hieroglyphics of pain.

She was the ghost.
She haunted me every night
ranting and raving
because of the ghosts
that haunted her.

Mirrors

She lives in a world
where it's fine
to opt out of adolescence,
to step out
to find a worm
to eat.

The world of the rich is like that,
bills are the best make-up
for a blemish,
ask any private school
to molest your money
and give your gal a gorgeous grade,
they'll do it,

but in the end
the canopy constructed
to cuddle your cousin from 9-3 collapses,

nighttime comes
and the stars hold
their million mirrors up
to the charade.

Dwarfed

The smallest one
is four inches,
can be carried
in one hand,
as delicate as a china doll,
but not as easy to manage.

People prefer
the six to eight inch ones
which can be trained and styled
without much trouble.

The more control the gardener has
the better.

Constant Chronic

An established bonsai
requires dwarfing—
to be planted in a shallow container
to suppress the growth of roots,
 to be placed on a shelf
with sufficient sunlight,
but insufficient water
and fertilizer;

mother will be happy
to comply.
To keep you small and stunted means
you will be wholly dependent
on her constant, chronic care.

In the Oven

Soil
formed on weathered rocks—
a complex system
of solids, liquids, gases,
supposedly feeds the children well,

how many bonsai
wilt and wither
because the watering
 involves such patience?

The wounded roots
must be pruned,
their cuts wrapped
in sphagnum moss,

although mothers
are busy
baking.

Broken Bonsais

Bitch of a bonsai gardener
wants to clip my branches.
I have been here before.

I would rather die
than be pruned,
pampered,
perfect as a pedigree.

I would bruise the roots
she's audacious enough
to call hands,
if I could
I would.
Believe me.

Schizophrenic Mother

When I was five
I walked arm-in-arm
with my mother
down Main Street, Flushing,
past Klein's Department Store,
Gertz, some diners, a bakery.
Her hand felt slimy
and her eyes looked like they were
 falling out of her sockets.

If I saw a friend
off in the distance,
I'd quickly break loose
from her embrace,
run off into the crowd
make believe I was shopping
by myself.

Spring Burials

In sleep
I unpetal you,
each layer
of rich, red leaf
waves to the wind
till there is nothing
but the stalk, the stamen
the pollen locked within.

I need to free
the pollen from the casket.

Wounds: A Found Poem *

Trees that grow on mountains
or island rocks,
exposed to strong winds and snow,
enduring earthquakes
and the pressure from the land for years,
have gnarled and twisted trunks.

Some heal
over with knots,
while others
swell or hollow.

*THE LIVING ART OF BONSAI (134)

Breeders

Bugs that breed bountifully
and batter bonsais,
are nature's cry
to mama,
"Ha.
Ha, ha.
I grow and reproduce rapidly
robbing you
of your budding blossoms
you thought you could keep perfect
forever."

Damage

Can't wait till spring
when I, sleeping insect ,
awaken
reproduce rapidly
and prepare for war.

When I do battle with mother
she loses,
since I'm immune to toxic chemicals
and the control
she thinks she has.

My dangerously damaged gene
is dormant
in cold, winter months,
waiting.
Just waiting.

Against the Wall

She didn't mean to murder her baby,
but she did.

She meant
to be a good mother
not the one
who snaps the neck of a baby bird.

She was bruised,
she was battered,
forty foster homes
in four years.

She swore
not to be the mother
who abandons her daughter
on the stoop,

so she smashed her against the wall
instead.

Coiled Style

Alarming
the way the roots
spread out in every direction—
an octopus
with a completely twisted base.

The tree tapers toward the top
like a shaved head,
though the branches
are agreeably balanced,

but the trunk
is gnarled
from years of abuse
at the hands of an angry mountain.

Military General Style 11

A snake-like trunk,
two main branches
extending arms,
five to seven layers
of horizontal growth,
and a mother
who has a manual of rules
 which, when disobeyed,
decides
to strangle
the already delicate
and damaged roots.

Cascade Style: A Partially Found Poem *

Trees that grow
on precipitous mountains
broken ridges of cliffs,
and are exposed
to severe snowstorms
or other inclement weather,
cling precariously
to the ledges of rocks above precipices.

In order to gain
more sunlight and space,
they struggle
to stretch out their branches
as if they're grasping for some unknown
while hanging, hungrily
over the edge of cliffs.

*THE LIVING ART OF BONSAI (133)

ICU

So easy to die,
not just
the heart-like rocks
that keep the limbs in place,
but the endless tubing
its sustenance.
So difficult to water
if one wire moves.

This bonsai
is smaller then the rest.
(what you don't know
is the mother never watered it,
swallowed ammonia
used a hanger)
everything
but a tree doctor
to get rid of the thing
she knew would be deformed.

Now
look—
it will never grow
and everyone will know
just how mama feels.

Dead Dancers

That bonsai
is a ballerina
on point.
The stage is soil,
the movement, still
like a Degas
of dead dancers
who hide their faces
from the light,
the artist's choice
of where to grow
or not to.

.

Wiring

Wiring
changes the direction
of the trunk and branches;
growth can be
suppressed by these wires
to create a new apex.

What a shame
for the buds
that have been beckoned elsewhere.

Rules for Repotting

But the wire
is necessary,
so is the water.
Too wet
the roots may rot.
Too dry,
not enough moisture.

Tell me how
to create a tree child
without any rules
for repotting.

Rot in Peace

I have a "bonsai beauty,"
I have had her
for sixteen years.

Lately
(after the discharge showed up
on the leaf),

she's different..
They say water, wiring,
correct care
will work,

what happens
when the shape of the tree changes?
(so they say
it's not supposed to),

you know
you're doing your best
to mend the abrasions,

but the limbs
the way they contort
so spastically
tell you—

stay away.
Do not touch.

Losses

The shape
of ache and longing
is your leaf
loping downward
like an old lady
who has already left
her life.

Cloak of Invisibility

The bonsais are fading
in a cloak of invisibility;
there's a new tree
that's the style.
Bonsais
are now old people
called, "sweetheart"
because they once were beautiful,
although it's been awhile.
Now their limbs are palsied,
their green skin
 withered and waterless.

Hurricane Andrew

Imagine
your baseball cards
your bed
your room
swallowed by the wind;

you almost lost your mother
in the debris,
but then you found her.

Now they tell you:
here's a can of beans—
eat it;
a cot—
sleep on it,

but when darkness comes
all you do is sit and stare
eyes like empty pages.

If you close them
everything may disappear.

Emergency Treatment for Over-Fertilization:
A Found Poem *

The key
to fertilizing
is to feed the tree frequently,
but sparingly.
No strong fertilizers!

In case a strong fertilizer is used
and the roots burn,
immerse the tree in a pail of water
for two to three hours.
Then remove
and move it
to a shady and cool place.

If the damage is serious
immediate pruning, transplanting
and repotting
are necessary.

*THE LIVING ART OF BONSAI (188)

Correcting Defects of Roots: A Partially Found Poem *

1. Crooked, curled, entangled or vertical roots can be severed or corrected with wires, pebbles or pieces of bamboo.
2. Cut stems short as early as possible to ensure growth of fine roots.
3. Roots can also be created by height layering.
4. Roots will thicken quickly when exposed to sunlight.

If all else fails
give up,
hide your head in the sand
as you have
been doing forever.

You created this mess,
now live with it.

*THE LIVING ART OF BONSAI (228)

Hunger
To Addie

Picture your child
walking into a 7-11
clutching her tattered limbs
just bruised
by the man
who raped her,
her mother, her brother
and killed the other two.

She's been left in the forest
alone,
so she wanders out

to this safe store
where people pass her
without a question
or a clue.

Imagine what's in her head, this child
who has no fairy godmother,
not even a witch
to rescue her.

Imagine her hunger
this July 4th
when you're at your barbecue
and four beautifully tanned children

 one at a time
jump off the high-diving board,

while you imagine
they know how to swim.

A Tale

Unlatch
the wires
that have held her in beauty
too long.

(Didn't the Chinese princess
whose feet were bound and bleeding
but delicate and brilliant
once ask
for the bandages to be broken?)

I thought I heard this tale—
a Chinese princess
damned by her beauty.

So is this bonsai
eager to grow,
ready to be rid of the rewards
of its perfect shape,

but the master—
the empress
the mother roots
have dug their ugly claws,

and are not about
to let go.
Not now.
Not ever.

The Cape

I remember
the day I bought the cape,
and swirled like a dolphin
deliciously in the air.

I was happy
to wear a wardrobe
others had.
Fifteen and finally
normal.

The next day
friends
joined the parade of capes,
their rainbow of colors
flashing and flaunting,

while I
lamented the loss
of that moment
when I marched to their music,

but my stepmother
had made me buy beige—
dull, pale,
able, like the earth

to sink lower and lower
to hide beneath the cape
of the ground.

Bare and Blistered

I try on shoes
the way Goldilocks tried three chairs
to find the right fit,

nothing works!
even though
shoes crawl out of my closet
like an ant invasion.

I would like to say,
there's one black, satin pair
I have loved too wisely and well,
or a glass slipper
that fits perfectly,

but I am afraid
at the end of the tale
with all the loafers, oxfords,
platforms, pumps
suffocating my battered feet,

that I'll still run into the forest
bare and blistered.

The Other Story of Hansel and Gretel

There is an unsuspecting witch in the forest
the mother too good
to be true.

Her home
is better than gingerbread.
It's filled with fruits and vegetables
(candy, too!).

Everything is delicious
because this mother
is a gourmet cook.
Her stews simmer on the stove
from morning till night.

The older sister knows this,
tucked comfortably in her cashmere blanket,
silk sheets on the bed
two fluffy pillows.

She knows this
since she sniffs
the wonderful smells
wafting through the house
like a dream.

This bigger girl, the adolescent
drifts in and out of dreams
and of sickness.
She's been sick for years.
She's missed school
and adolescence,
but she doesn't mind
she likes it here;
it's comfortable and cozy.

The younger child
(boy or girl?)

not certain of its sex
with hair as short as grass,

has been neutered,
doesn't smile,
but doesn't cry either.

The younger child comes home
to dark rooms
and dangerously daring meals.

She or he will eat, do homework,
hide upstairs,
while the teenage sister
listens to the songs of salvation
sighing from her mother's lips.

She will never leave
this mother, this oven.

Her mother has mentioned
the monsters outside
and she believes her.

II.

Out of the Museum, Into the World

Bleeding Bonsais

I am bleeding bonsais
since I've turned fifty,
they seep
through my sleep
like some genie
generous enough
to have granted me
in my middle years—
great beauty,
good children
the secrets of silence and wisdom
enough to know
whatever tree I have
is good enough.

Dear Hades,

You thought
if I kept my eyes closed
for a long time
I'd embrace your world,
and all its wretched darkness;
for years
I believed in the power of geotropism—
I sucked in your slimy smells,
the dampness of your soils,
and forgot—
the sun,
the skies,
the trees.

Until one day
I was the beanstalk
fantastic phototropism
I leaped
to the light
like Persephone only does in springtime.

I am the whole in the sunflower
that never gets eaten.

Solitude

This was a sad poem;
this was a mutated tree,

until it decided
to find a river
droop its head low
and scoop moonlight off of water,
leave the land.

Now it is a happy poem
a plant that understands
shifting shadows may mean
no sunlight today.

But it is better
to be planted
where no tree
has ever grown before

than to be
stuck in soil

so beautiful
rich and dark,
but rotten
to the core.

Locket

Tree and pot
should complement each other
like a locket
holding the picture of a lover
for everyone to admire.

The Abortion

It would be simple
to expel you.

In my grandmother's days
they used wire hangers,
while some girls
jumped up and down
certain
there'd be an accident.

I could walk
into a white-washed room
where a smiling doctor
wearing rubber gloves
could pinch and prod you

till you'd emerge
without finger or toenails,

but with hands as tiny as ladybugs
and legs, curled
like a hemorrhaged rose.

In the Womb: Hearing a Baby's Heart Beat for the First Time

Like a dream
not sure of where it's going,
but enjoying itself too much
to awaken you,

it throbs
beneath the surface
as if noises

are bubbling
out of a swamp.
Such delicate threads
out of this luscious mud

that you wish
this were forever
this moment

when this splendid child
first let you know
I am.

The Most Magnificent Tree

The material
is collected
from the mountains.
The best trees
come from shallow, poor sandy
or sometimes sunny areas,
which shows you
you can produce shrubs
similar to mother,
yet sometimes
from the worst stock
comes the most magnificent tree.

My Backyard

I am not a bonsai,
nor a maple, an elm,
a redwood,
there is no forest for me

I am free
of green and rust and red,
but not dead.

I am a plant that grows
its own toe-
like roots,
discovers
saturated soil,
but only for a while
before I leave.

Don't look me up
in the plant dictionary.
Don't send me for an MA,

I'm not interested in mothers
or groups,
only
in archaeology,
which, I am happy to say
is abundant
in my own backyard.

Forests

The orthodox women
don't buy bonsais,
they prefer
to walk with the maple
simple as the Sabbath.

These women
water their children
with food
that isn't fake,

so many children
in their home,

but not one bonsai,
they are beautiful
nevertheless,
grow tall
and gorgeous
stick together
like a lush, green forest.

Shaping

It's art
creating bonsai.
It depends on
the manipulation by man,
but what about nature
forging its own course,
no training, shaping, sculpting,
just roots
with abundant room
to discover
the kind of tree
it wants to be.

Propagation

Scions
from superior bonsai
can be grafted
to stocks of the same species
so favorable characteristics
of the parent tree
can be reproduced in the new one,

but the Japanese red maple
depends on grafting
since this helps it
to grow faster
than a parent tree;

how fortunate
since a plant should always be better
or at least different
from its parent.

Far Away in the World

A tree with an even root base
will have balanced and uniform
growth above the ground,
then its branches, foliage and buds
will be beautiful,
at which point
I tell my children
grow somewhere else
far away in the world.

Branches

Without a trunk
a tree can have no branches,
without branches
the tree will not develop
a beautiful line.
The goal is to recreate
the beauty
of an aged tree;

yet I am telling you, child
dream your own dreams.
You don't need
to sleep with mine.

Cross Country Skiing, Pound Ridge, February, 1988

In these woods
it's hard to know
where clouds end
and land begins,
hard to know
where I end
my long, hard tracks
and you begin,
your tiny, gentle ones,
and whose voice
is moving the branches—
the wind
or your three year old breathful sounds?
Where are the edges,
drifting, drifting
your footsteps in my footsteps
in the lullaby
of snow.

Procedure for Transplanting: A Partially Found Poem*
To Craig, Twenty

1. Prepare a pot of suitable shape, size and color
2. Cover the draining holes with plastic mesh to prevent loss of soil
3. Prepare a good soil mix that is compatible with the tree species and the size of the pot.
4. Tell your son, though it's not in the manual:
   A. Find fresh, new soil.
   B. Cut away the roots.
   C. Race to the finish line.

*THE LIVING ART OF BONSAI (245)

Magic: A Mother's Prayer

I dreamed
God made me a magician,
so that I could grant him five inches
muscles, a mustache
anything
to make him feel like a man;

though he is a man
he is everything
a man should be—
handsome, smart
as kind as a spring wind
and warm, too;

dear God,
if magic
can't make him a redwood
at least
zap him fearless as a tree
bold, brazen with bush
dangling his leaves
like wild flags
in 2 A.M. darkness.

The Vast Forest
To Craig, Twenty

It is better
to choose a tree
with steady growth patterns
so its branches
will not elongate and thicken abruptly;
it should have
auxiliary buds,
be thornless,
have fine twigs
and short internodes;
this is the way you grow an evergreen
with lustrous green leaves.

My beautiful son
please race out of the pot
and soon,
a vast forest
awaits you.

Sun Set

"Come see the sun," I shout
watching it slip behind the cloud
like a thief,

but the son
is not interested.
At fifteen
he has better things to watch—breasts, bikinis,
barely-clothed girls;
this is why he came to Hawaii.

The green primordial fields
shimmering in volcanic cauldrons;
the ocean gushing,
foaming at the mouth
rising erect as a stalk;
who cares about the scenery
with the bodies, beautiful bodies.

The sun, now covered in total darkness,
but these bodies
set splendor in the sky.

Fragrance
To Samantha, Sixteen

My flower
you are the fragrance
that fills the room
with longing;

mine, for youth
yours to pollinate
and powder the world
with your passion

Braces

The braces
like a picket fence
have held the hands of others
in a harness
for so long,

but once they come off
there is no protection
for those lush, green leaves
and flowering petals

because this mother
doesn't want her bonsai daughter
locked in a museum.

Satsuki Azalea
To Samantha Rose, Sixteen

You are my satsuki azalea,
the fruitful fragrance,
thick petals and long, flowering period,
plus
the female plants bloom
more easily than the male.
You pollinate so easily,
pink buds blush
brazenly.

I am blessed
you are mine,
still I will depot you
and let you go.

A Yoga Lesson
To my fourteen year old daughter

Dearest daughter,

Do you feel my hand
a cushion
beneath your back?

When you bend
into bridge pose
does your torso belong
bent over backwards?

Do you mind
taking yoga
with your mom?

I finger
your flesh
in child's pose

curled
into the garden of the self,
suddenly
a woman's body
breathing heavy, meditative breaths;

the hum
of desire
hidden in tree posture
poised upward.

Will the branch break
away-away-away
only to return
in another form?

Downward in Desire

I found a high stand
for your branches
flowing downward
in desire,
my weeping daughter
bonsai,
do not cry
for I want you to escape.

That is why
I have cared for you
so well.

On the Eve of Halloween
To Samantha, Five

When the clothes come off,
when darkness descends
darker than ever,
and the ghosts and goblins come out;
when sleep comes
a gift God has given
and the costume lies like a heap on the floor—
a Beauty costume
with no one to fill it,
that's when you are beautiful,
sleeping, naked
all five years
filled with dreams
that Halloween be every day,

while my treat
is watching you
asleep.

A Fairy-Tale of Three Mothers

One was mean and ugly
they wouldn't even call her
a witch;
hag was better,
but even that
wasn't enough
since her outside was only moderately ugly,
but her insides
were brutal.
Not only did she scream,
she howled like a werewolf,
and I was scared of being bitten
though in truth
she only hit
sometimes pulled my hair,
and screamed profanities
out to the wind.
I got rid of her
as soon as I possibly could.

I found a pretty mother,
pretty, but dumb.
I didn't know she was dumb
until she forgot to make me dinner
or bring me to school,
but she didn't scream
and bought me beautiful clothes
from Bloomingdale's.

I discarded the clothes
kept the mother,
realizing
she was sometimes purposeful,
but mostly
I viewed myself as orphaned
until I had children
and found myself another mother
besides myself

for them.

She was fat and gruesome,
but kind and wholesome
and never cursed
only said "stupid" sometimes.

But when I peeked behind her words,
I realized how the world
was stupid in her eyes,
and dark and ugly.

It was too long before I realized
this mother cooked a wicked brew
that I wasn't about to drink.

So now I am through with mothers.
I'm throwing them out
into the brambles and branches
of some terribly dark woods,
while I, on the other hand,
have discovered the exit from the forest
and am lusting and mothering
in the light.

The Imperial Mother
To Ira

How fortunate
to have escaped the forest
without a surface scratch.

Oh, there are bruises, for sure
but the black and blue
that billows inside,
is invisible to the eye.

Nor can anyone gaze
at the mother
who cast me, alone,
into the woods.
She's in an institution
in a harness
like a horse
ready to be put down.

But once upon a time
this mother screamed,
"God is dead
you little bitch.
Leave my kingdom
Immediately."
The voices of the king
commanded her.

The moral of this tale
is I was never trapped
in the brambles and branches
of the spastic trees
too long,

and when I came out
the light was lovely
I learned to lavish my children in it,
to feed them abundantly,

to be willing to abdicate the throne
because my prince and princess
have grown up
with a dove
with which they can fly.

ABOUT THE AUTHOR

Pamela L. Laskin is a lecturer in the English Department, where she directs the Poetry Outreach Center. Poetry collections include: *Remembering Fireflies* and *Secrets of Sheets* (Plain View Press), *Van Gogh's Ear* (Červená Barva Press), Daring Daughter's/Defiant Dreams (A Gathering of Tribes), and *The Plagiarist* (Dos Madres Press). Several children's books have been published.

www.ingramcontent.com/pod-product-compliance
Lightning Source LLC
Chambersburg PA
CBHW031005090426
42737CB00008B/682

9780988371354